Let's Read About Our Bodies
Conozcamos nuestro cuerpo

Eyes/Ojos

Cynthia Klingel & Robert B. Noyed
photographs by/fotografías por Gregg Andersen

Reading consultant/Consultora de lectura: Cecilia Minden-Cupp, Ph.D.,
Adjunct Professor, College of Continuing and Professional Studies, University of Virginia

Weekly Reader.
EARLY LEARNING LIBRARY

For a free color catalog describing Weekly Reader® Early Learning Library's list of high-quality books, call 1-800-542-2595 or fax your request to (414) 332-3567.

Library of Congress Cataloging-in-Publication Data

Klingel, Cynthia.
    Eyes = Ojos / by Cynthia Klingel and Robert B. Noyed. — [Bilingual ed.]
      p. cm. — (Let's read about our bodies = Conozcamos nuestro cuerpo)
    Includes bibliographical references and index.
    Summary: A bilingual introduction to eyes, what they are used for, and how to take care of them.
    ISBN 0-8368-3072-5 (lib. bdg.)
    1. Eye—Juvenile literature. [1. Eye. 2. Vision. 3. Senses and sensation. 4. Spanish
language materials—Bilingual.] I. Title: Ojos. II. Noyed, Robert B. III. Title.
QM511.K56   2002
612.8'4—dc21   2001055089

This edition first published in 2002 by
Weekly Reader® Early Learning Library
330 West Olive Street, Suite 100
Milwaukee, WI 53212 USA

Copyright © 2002 by Weekly Reader® Early Learning Library

An Editorial Directions book
Editors: E. Russell Primm and Emily Dolbear
Translators: Tatiana Acosta and Guillermo Gutiérrez
Art direction, design, and page production: The Design Lab
Photographer: Gregg Andersen
Weekly Reader® Early Learning Library art direction: Tammy West
Weekly Reader® Early Learning Library page layout: Katherine A. Goedheer

All rights reserved. No part of this book may be reproduced, stored in a retrieval system, or transmitted in any form or by any means, electronic, mechanical, photocopying, recording, or otherwise without the prior written permission of the copyright holder.

Printed in the United States of America

4 5 6 7 8 9 10 09 08 07 06

Note to Educators and Parents

As a Reading Specialist I know that books for young children should engage their interest, impart useful information, and motivate them to want to learn more.

Let's Read About Our Bodies is a new series of books designed to help children understand the value of good health and of taking care of their bodies.

A young child's active mind is engaged by the carefully chosen subjects. The imaginative text works to build young vocabularies. The short, repetitive sentences help children stay focused as they develop their own relationship with reading. The bright, colorful photographs of children enjoying good health habits complement the text with their simplicity to both entertain and encourage young children to want to learn – and read – more.

These books are designed to be used by adults as "read-to" books to share with children to encourage early literacy in the home, school, and library. They are also suitable for more advanced young readers to enjoy on their own.

Una nota a los educadores y a los padres

Como especialista en lectura, sé que los libros infantiles deben interesar a los niños, proporcionar información útil y motivarlos a aprender.

Conozcamos nuestro cuerpo es una nueva serie de libros pensada para ayudar a los niños a entender la importancia de la salud y del cuidado del cuerpo.

Los temas, cuidadosamente seleccionados, mantienen ocupada la activa mente del niño. El texto, lleno de imaginación, facilita el enriquecimiento del vocabulario infantil. Las oraciones, breves y repetitivas, ayudan a los niños a centrarse en la actividad mientras desarrollan su propia relación con la lectura. Las bellas fotografías de niños que disfrutan de buenos hábitos de salud complementan el texto con su sencillez, y consiguen entretener a los niños y animarlos a aprender nuevos conceptos y a leer más.

Estos libros están pensados para que los adultos se los lean a los niños, con el fin de fomentar la lectura incipiente en el hogar, en la escuela y en la biblioteca. También son adecuados para que los jóvenes lectores más avanzados los disfruten leyéndolos por su cuenta.

Cecilia Minden-Cupp, Ph.D., Adjunct Professor,
College of Continuing and Professional Studies, University of Virginia

These are my eyes.
I have two eyes.

- - - - - - -

Éstos son mis ojos.
Tengo dos ojos.

Eyes can be many colors.

- - - - - - -

Los ojos pueden ser de muchos colores.

I use my eyes to see.
I can see big things
and small things.

Uso los ojos para ver.
Puedo ver cosas grandes
y cosas pequeñas.

I use my eyes to see
things that are far away.

- - - - - - - -

Uso los ojos para ver
cosas que están lejos.

I use my eyes to see
things that are close.

- - - - - - - -

Uso los ojos para ver
cosas que están cerca.

Sometimes we need glasses to help us see better.

– – – – – – –

A veces necesitamos lentes para ver mejor.

I need to keep my eyes clean and safe. I never put things in my eyes!

Tengo que limpiarme los ojos y cuidarlos. ¡Nunca me meto nada en los ojos!

I wear sunglasses
when it is bright outside.

- - - - - - -

Llevo lentes oscuros
cuando hace mucho sol.

My eyes work hard
all day. My eyes rest
at night.

- - - - - - -

Mis ojos trabajan mucho
todo el día. Mis ojos
descansan por la noche.

Glossary/Glosario

bright—filled with light
soleado—lleno de luz del sol

clean—free from dirt
limpio—sin suciedad

safe—free from harm or danger
cuidar—proteger de daños o peligros

sunglasses—dark eyeglasses that protect the eyes from the sun
lentes oscuros—lentes que protegen los ojos de la luz del sol

For More Information/Más información

Fiction Books/Libros de ficción

Brown, Eric. *Arthur's Eyes*. Boston: Little, Brown & Co., 1983.

Seuss, Dr. *The Eye Book*. New York: Random House, 1999.

Smith, Lane. *Glasses: Who Needs 'Em?* New York: Viking, 1991.

Nonfiction Books/Libros de no ficción

Ballard, Carol. *How Do Our Eyes See?* Austin, Tex.: Raintree/Steck-Vaughn, 1998.

Fowler, Allan. *How Animals See Things*. Danbury, Conn.: Children's Press, 1999.

Jedrosz, Aleksander. *Eyes*. Mahwah, N.J.: Troll, 1992.

Web Sites/Páginas Web

A Big Look at the Eye

kidshealth.org/kid/body/eye_SW.html

For more information about the way the eye works

Index/Índice

About the Authors/Información sobre los autores

Cynthia Klingel has worked as a high school English teacher and an elementary school teacher. She is currently the curriculum director for a Minnesota school district. Cynthia Klingel lives with her family in Mankato, Minnesota.

Cynthia Klingel ha trabajado como maestra de inglés de secundaria y como maestra de primaria. Actualmente es la directora de planes de estudio de un distrito escolar de Minnesota. Cynthia Klingel vive con su familia en Mankato, Minnesota.

Robert B. Noyed started his career as a newspaper reporter. Since then, he has worked in school communications and public relations at the state and national level. Robert B. Noyed lives with his family in Brooklyn Center, Minnesota.

Robert B. Noyed comenzó su carrera como reportero en un periódico. Desde entonces ha trabajado en comunicación escolar y relaciones públicas a nivel estatal y nacional. Robert B. Noyed vive con su familia en Brooklyn Center, Minnesota.